KV-050-573

PIZZA

UNIVERSITY OF
INFORMATION
SERVICES
CENTRAL ENGLAND

Favourite Foods

Cake
Chips
Chocolate
Ice-Cream
Milkshake
Pizza

UNIVERSITY OF
CENTRAL ENGLAND

Book no. 0798548 7

Subject no. 641 .8248 Mos

INFORMATION SERVICES

All words that appear in **bold** are explained in the glossary on page 30

First published in 1992 by
Wayland (Publishers) Ltd
61 Western Road, Hove
East Sussex BN3 1JD, England
© Copyright 1992 Wayland (Publishers) Ltd

Editor: Francesca Motisi
Research: Anne Moses

British Library Cataloguing in Publication Data
Moses, Brian
    Pizza.—(Favourite Foods Series)
    I. Title   II. Gordon, Mike   III. Series
    641.3

    ISBN 0-7502-0518-0

Typeset by Dorchester Typesetting Group Ltd
Printed and bound in Belgium by Casterman, S.A.

PIZZA

Written by Brian Moses

Illustrated by Mike Gordon

Wayland

Do you pick up your pizza at the supermarket,

. . . or phone for a number 5?

Do you visit a
pizza parlour,

. . . or make one yourself at home?

Did you know that when people lived in caves they ate pizzas? They used red-hot stones to bake the round discs of bread that we use in pizzas today.

The **Romans** enjoyed pizzas too. They added cheese, tomatoes and **herbs**, and ate their pizzas for breakfast!

Now, let's see how pizzas are made today.

To begin with, the wheat is harvested, then milled and ground into flour.

FLOUR

8

This is taken to a factory and mixed with **yeast** and water.
The mixture is then **kneaded** together to make **dough**.

The dough is rolled flat and over 400 pizza bases are stamped out every minute. These are baked and cooled.

The bases now pass through three
different 'waterfalls' of sauce,
cheese and topping.

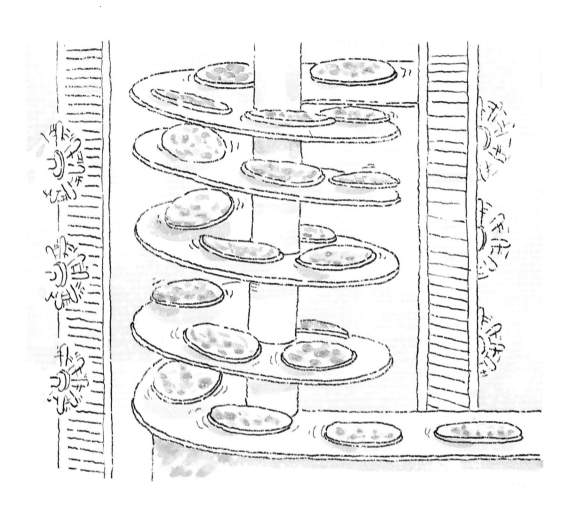

Then the pizzas are frozen in a spiral
blast freezer.

Finally, they are wrapped in clear
cellophane and packed into
bags or cartons.

Ingredients for pizzas come from all over

the world.

The chewy cheese topping
may be Mozzarella.
This comes from Italy.
When it is cooked
it stretches like
chewing gum.

Tinned chopped tomatoes
come from Italy too.

Olives  may come from

Portugal,  hot **chillis**

from Mexico,  green or red

peppers  from Spain,

slices of banana

 from Jamaica

and sultanas from sunny
California in the USA.

Italian restaurants often have special ovens for cooking pizzas. These ovens are so hot that the pizzas cook really quickly. This means that the pizzas are piping hot for the customers.

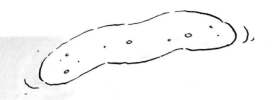

Expert pizza-makers throw the dough
up into the air . . . and then catch it.

If you try this at home . . . it could turn out rather messy!

This group of children are about
to make a quick and easy pizza.
They are washing their hands well
before starting.

If you make this at home you will need
some help from an adult, especially
when cutting with a sharp knife and
using the oven.

For the topping you will need:

400g (14oz) can of chopped tomatoes
1/2 a small onion
a pinch of pepper and salt
50g–75g (2–3oz) of grated cheese
a dessert spoon of tomato purée
a dessert spoon of cornflour
some mixed herbs

For the base you will need:

150g (6oz) of self-raising flour
(can be 4oz brown and 2oz white)
40g (1$\frac{1}{2}$ oz) margarine
1 egg
milk to mix

This is what you do:

Ask an adult to help make this recipe.

1 Switch oven on at 220°C (425°F) Gas mark 7.

 **2** Peel and chop onion and put in saucepan.

3 Add tomatoes, herbs and purée – stir well, then heat and leave to simmer for 10 minutes. Stir occasionally.

4 Put cornflour in a cup with enough cold water to mix to a paste. Stir in 2 or 3 spoons of hot tomato liquid. Now pour back into the saucepan and heat sauce for another 5 minutes.

5 As sauce cooks and cools, lightly grease a shallow flan dish. Sieve together brown and white flour with the pinch of salt.

6 Cut margarine into flour and then rub in with fingertips.

7 When mixture looks like breadcrumbs, mix in the egg and add enough milk to make mixture stick together.

8 Put dough into flan dish and press gently so that it covers the base.

9 Now cover with the tomato sauce topping and grated cheese. Bake in the oven for 20-25 minutes until edges are looking golden brown.

Make a face pattern with olives,
mushrooms and slices of cheese, or
ham, cut into shapes. Use strips of
green pepper for eyebrows.

Pizza

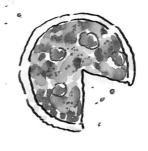

I love to bite
a chewy slice
of gooey pizza,
it's really nice.

The tomatoey taste
and cheesy topping,
always get
my taste buds popping.

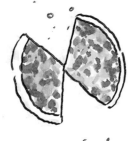

Sliced or whole
it suits my mood,
pizza is really
my favourite food!

Italy is the home of pizzas, but now you can get them all over the world. Maybe you could enter your pizza in the Best Pizza In The World Competition, held in **Rimini**.

Glossary

Chillis Small red or green peppers which are very hot to taste.

Dough The uncooked mixture of flour, water and sometimes yeast, which is baked into bread and cakes.

Herbs Plants used in cooking to give food a better flavour. Basil and oregano are often used in pizzas.

Kneaded Moulded together with your fingers. In pizza-making the dough is kneaded.

Olives The black or green fruit of the olive tree.

Rimini A town on the north-east coast of Italy.

Romans The people who lived in ancient Rome about 2000 years ago. The Romans also invaded Britain and lived here for over 450 years.

Simmer To heat something gently and keep it just below boiling point.

Yeast A type of fungus, used to make bread rise.

Acknowledgements
The author and publisher would like to thank McCain Foods (G.B.) Limited for their advice on pizza production.

Notes for parents and teachers

Read the book with children, either individually or in groups. Who has eaten pizzas? When and where? Ask for comments about the illustrations as you turn each page. What are children's favourite toppings? What do they know about Italy – the home of the pizza?

Write about pizzas – My perfect pizza would be . . . Find out about various kinds of cheese, what they look like and where they come from. Write about them and draw pictures.

Suggest that children bring to school empty pizza packets. Talk about the ingredients. Are there items in these pizzas that haven't been mentioned in this book? How much do the pizzas cost and how much does each one weigh? Which is the best value?

Ask children to collect advertisements from pizza takeaways. These are sometimes found slipped inside free papers or posted through letterboxes. Talk about the various choices. Design menu cards and then ask older children to order pizzas for their families. Can they work out the total cost of each meal? Swap these with other children for checking.

Some children may enjoy designing pretend pizzas on cardboard or plastic plates. Discuss what materials will be needed and make a list of them before they begin. Who can design the most interesting looking pizza? Hold a BEST PIZZA IN THE CLASS COMPETITION.

Children who attempt the recipe will be finding similarities and differences in a variety of cooking materials. They will discover how food changes when cooked e.g. cheese melts, flour, margarine, milk and egg will make dough which can be moulded and then flattened. Dough will also have a different appearance when it is cooked.

Children should also be able to talk about what they have done and to remember the order in which they prepared their pizzas. Simple flow charts and diagrams could be produced by older children to show the stages in the recipe and also the stages in the production of factory pizzas.

The above suggestions will satisfy a number of statements of attainment in National Curriculum guidelines for English, Maths and Science at Key Stage 1.

Books to read

A Packet of Poems – Poems about food, selected by
Jill Bennett (OUP 1982)
A Picnic of Poetry – selected by Anne Harvey
(Blackie 1988/Puffin 1990)
Bread by Christine Butterworth (Hodder & Stoughton,
1990)
You and Your Child: Kitchen Fun by Ray Gibson
(Usborne, 1990)
The Usborne First Cook Book by Angela Wilkes &
Stephen Cartwright (Usborne, 1987)

Index